BRUCE LEE'S
FIGHTING METHOD

BRUCE LEE'S
FIGHTING METHOD

ADVANCED TECHNIQUES

by

BRUCE LEE and **M. UYEHARA**

Poetry by Mike Plane

OHARA 🔲 PUBLICATIONS, INCORPORATED

SANTA CLARITA, CALIFORNIA

WARNING

BRUCE LEE–1940-1973

Bruce Lee flashed brilliantly like a meteor through the world of martial arts and motion pictures. Then, on July 20, 1973, in Hong Kong, like a meteor—he vanished, extinguished by sudden death. He was just 32.

Bruce Lee began his martial arts studies with wing chun, under the tutelage of the late Yip Man, to alleviate the personal insecurity instilled by Hong Kong city life. Perhaps because his training enveloped him to the point of fanaticism, he was eventually able to refine, distill and mature into a philosopher, technician and innovator of the martial arts.

After intensive study of different martial arts styles and theories, Lee developed a concept of martial arts for the individual man. This concept he later labeled Jeet Kune Do, the way of the intercepting fist. It has antecedents not only in his physical training and voluminous martial arts library (over two thousand books), but in his formal education as well (a philosophy major at the University of Washington, Seattle).

Lee also combined his martial arts expertise with his knowledge of acting skills and cinematic techniques, starring in several motion pictures: *The Big Boss*, *Fists of Fury*, *Way of the Dragon* and *Enter the Dragon*.

Bruce Lee's death plunged both martial arts and film enthusiasts into an abyss of disbelief. Out of their growing demand to know more of and about him, his *Tao of Jeet Kune Do* was published—which is now followed by BRUCE LEE'S FIGHTING METHOD.

This fourth in a series of volumes, which has been compiled and organized by his longtime friend, M. Uyehara, utilizes some of the many thousands of pictures from Lee's personal photo files. Uyehara is a former student of Bruce Lee.

DEDICATION

To all the friends and students of Bruce Lee

ACKNOWLEDGEMENT

Our sincere appreciation to Joe Bodner, who spent so much time in photographing and developing the film. Our appreciation also goes to those who participated in this book: Dan Inosanto and Ted Wong. They were both Bruce Lee's devoted students.

To Rainbow Publications, Inc., for the use of several photographs taken by Oliver Pang.

Introduction

This book was in the making in 1966 and most of the photographs were shot then. The late Bruce Lee intended to publish this book years ago but decided against it when he learned that martial arts instructors were using his name to promote themselves. It was quite common to hear comments like: "I taught Bruce Lee" or "Bruce Lee taught me jeet kune do." And Bruce may never have seen or known these martial artists.

Bruce didn't want people to use his name to promote themselves or their schools with false pretenses. He didn't want them to attract students this way, especially the young teens.

But after his death, his widow, Linda, felt that Bruce had contributed so much in the world of the martial arts that it would be a great loss if the knowledge of Bruce would die with him. Although the book can never replace the actual teaching and knowledge that Bruce Lee possessed, it will enhance you, the serious martial artist, in developing your skill in fighting.

Bruce always believed that all martial artists train diligently for one single purpose—to defend themselves. Whether we are in judo, karate, aikido, kung fu, etcetera, our ultimate goal is to prepare ourselves for any situation.

To train yourself for this goal, you must train seriously. Nothing is taken for granted. "You have to kick or punch the bag with concentrated efforts," Bruce used to say. "If you are going to train without the concept that this is the real thing, you are short-changing yourself. When you kick or punch the bag, you have to imagine that you are actually hitting an adversary. Really concentrating, putting 100 percent in your kicks and punches, is the only way you are going to be good."

If you have already read the other three volumes of *Bruce Lee's Fighting Method*, entitled *Self-Defense Techniques*, *Basic Training* and *Skill in Techniques*, you are now presented with the fourth and final book, *Advanced Techniques*. With this book you now have the only and complete set of lessons left by the late Bruce Lee. This volume, besides teaching you the more advanced fighting techniques, explains how to use your brains against your opponents; how to maneuver and what to do against different types of fighters; how to take the offensive and how to counterattack, etcetera. Almost all the photos in this book are being published here for the first time.

If you have not read *Tao of Jeet Kune Do* by Bruce Lee (Ohara Publications, Inc.), please read it. It was meant to complement this book, and the knowledge from both books will give you a full picture of Bruce's art.

Jeet Kune Do

Jeet Kune Do was founded by Bruce Lee
        because he felt
the martial arts were too confined.

You can't fight in pattern he used to say
        because an attack
can be baffling and not refined.

Jeet Kune Do was created by Bruce Lee
        to show us
that an old art must transform.

Like the day turns to night and
        night, to day
the way of fighting must also reform.

Bruce Lee developed Jeet Kune Do
        but wished
he didn't have a name for it!

Because the very words, Jeet Kune Do,
        already indicate
that it's another martial arts form.

Any form or style does restrict
and his belief is now in conflict.

Sources:
Tao of Jeet Kune Do by Bruce Lee
Boxing by Edwin L. Haislet

Contents

Chapter XII

Hand Techniques for Offense

(part 1)

Your Offense

Your offense should be simple and direct
because it may be hard to control.

But against someone who can project
a complex attack should be your role.

Timing, the key to a complex attack,
must be practiced until you have the knack.

The feint should be just enough to distract
and create an opening so you can act.

HAND TECHNIQUES FOR OFFENSE

In jeet kune do, there is hardly any direct attack. Practically all the offensive maneuvers are indirect—performed after a feint or in the form of a counterattack.

A perfect attack is the blending of strategy, speed, timing, deception and keen judgment. A superior fighter strives toward mastering all these elements in his daily training.

The attack should be launched at your own volition, upon your opponent's action or upon his inaction. For instance, a successful attack can be delivered when your opponent is withdrawing his arm from the path in which you intended to attack. In other words, attack when the line is open instead of closed. Your opponent is moving in the opposite direction and he must reverse his direction or alter it substantially, allowing you more time to succeed.

Simple attack will not always work against every opponent. You must learn to vary your attack and defense. This will bother your opponent but also help you cope with various styles of fighters.

You must study your opponent. Take advantage of his weaknesses and avoid his strengths. For instance, if your opponent is good at parrying, you should first use a press, feint or beat before attacking to confuse him in his parry.

The method of attacking is dictated by the form of defense. If your opponent is in your caliber, your attack can hardly be successful unless it outwits the defense. For instance, to deceive your opponent's hand defense, your hand offense is usually made of semi-circular or circular movements. But an offensive circular movement will not work if it is countered with a simple or lateral motion of a parry. Therefore, your stroke should be based upon your anticipation of the opponent's reaction.

It is precarious to attack with anything that comes to mind or to launch yourself into complicated compound attacks, allowing your opponent several chances for a stop-hit. The more complex the attack, the less your chance of executing it with control. Therefore, your attacks should be simple.

But if your opponent is equal in speed and in skill, with a good sense of distance, a simple attack may not score. Against such an opponent you have to use compound attack and take advantage of the distance.

Compound attack is a preliminary action such as a feint, beat, etcetera, before launching the real attack. The success of the compound attack depends directly on the parry of the feint or initial attack by your opponent. You have to study the opponent's reaction before applying the compound attack.

Compound attack depends on timing and opportunity. Many compound attacks fail because the attacker doesn't time his feints correctly. They should be moving just slightly before the real attack. Compound attacks can be short, fast combinations or deep, fast and penetrative combinations.

Simple compound attack—just one feint or one preliminary action—has a better chance to score if it is executed on the opponent's preparation, especially if he is stepping forward. Against an opponent who has slow feet or is exhausted, use the double lead.

In attacking, you should act and look boldly fierce as a wild animal to "psych" your opponent. You should attack with determination but not recklessly. It is risky to attack halfheartedly.

Even with good techniques, you can be frustrated by a skilled opponent's defensive measures. Therefore, you should time your attack perfectly so your opponent cannot evade your blows. Following are some of the hand techniques used in jeet kune do.

Leading Finger Jab

The leading finger jab, like the shin or knee side-kick, is the first line in offense or defense. It allows you an additional three or four

1

2

THE LEADING FINGER JAB

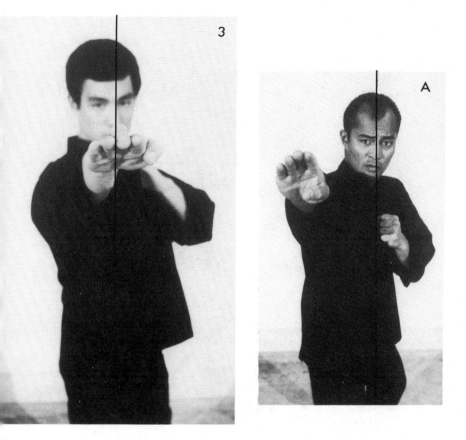

inches in reach and provides a fast strike because it travels only a short distance to the target.

Like other skilled movements, it must be practiced when you are fresh. Whenever you are fatigued, your tendency is to use sloppy motions for finesse and generalized efforts for specific ones. By using continuous sloppy movements, your proficiency is retarded and may even retrogress. Anytime you are exhausted, change your drill from skilled to endurance types of exercises.

The finger jab is executed from an on-guard position, as in photo 1. Just before thrusting, the fingers of your striking hand should be extended, as in photo 2. You should complete your strike directly in front of your nose, as in photo 3, and not like photo A, which leaves an opening at the upper line area.

To attack directly with a finger jab against a skilled fighter is quite difficult. Bruce Lee always used it with a feint first. For instance, in photo 1, Lee stands in the on-guard position as he faces his opponent, who is in a similar position. He then feints low by crouching slightly and moves forward as if to attack the opponent's midsection. This causes the opponent to lower his guarding or rear hand, as in photo 2. As soon as the opening develops, Lee quickly thrusts his fingers into the eye, as in photo 3.

Notice that Lee places his right foot next to the opponent's to prevent any retaliation from the opponent's foot. A feint is a preliminary motion to entice your opponent to react. You draw him to parry to a particular line and then you deliver an attack in another line or path.

Against an opponent with a left lead stance, as in photo A, Lee fakes with his right hand lead to lower the opponent's leading hand, as in photo B. In this instance, Lee is only concerned about the lead hand as it is obstructing his path to the target. Once the obstruction is removed, Lee quickly takes advantage with a quick thrust to his eye, as in photo C. In this attack, Lee is able to accomplish his technique from a farther distance. The feint can also be a low shin kick to disturb the opponent's composure.

Besides using it as a feint, it also prevents the opponent from delivering a kick.

Whether it is a jab, punch or kick, speed is so important when you want to lead him. You must have speed over your opponent and let him keep up or catch up to you.

Speed and timing should work together. You should be able to dictate the rhythm to your opponent by either speeding up or slowing down your movements. Another way is to establish a natural rhythm and then suddenly attack when your opponent is in the doldrums as his motion begins to drag.

Economy of motion and keeping your muscles flexible can increase your speed. A fault of most novice competitors is that they try too hard to finish the match quickly and begin to press and hasten the activity. This only makes them less effective as the tension causes unnecessary muscular contractions which act as brakes—reducing their speed and expending their energy.

A higher performance is obtained when an athlete is free and unrestrained, than when he tries to force or drive himself. When a runner is going as fast as he can, he should not feel that he ought to be going faster.

Another effective technique is to change your timing—slow down instead of speeding up your movement—just before impact. In other words, the launching of the strike has a moment of pause in its forward path, compelling your opponent to open the vulnerable line as he is thrown out of timing.

Timing may mean success or failure in your offensive and defensive techniques. The attack or counter should occur at the moment of your opponent's state of ineptitude. Attack should come when your opponent is engrossed in preparing his offense as he is momentarily concentrating more on attack than defense. Other opportune times are when there is an absence of touch, engaging or while changing in the engagement and when he is in motion—stepping forward, backward or side-by-side—because he cannot intuitively change direction until his action is completed.

It takes a great deal of concentration and practice to develop this awareness of your opponent's weak moment. You must also learn not to be trapped by a misleading, false rhythm emanated by a clever fighter.

Leading Straight Right

The leading straight is the "bread and butter" punch in jeet kune do. It is a reliable offensive weapon because the delivery is short, accurate and quick.

It can be a powerful blow if you twist your hips just a split-second before delivery. The blow should land in front of your nose, as in photo A and not like B. Your guard hand should be close to defend your head against any counterpunch. The blow should be directly at the face, as in photo C.

THE LEADING STRAIGHT RIGHT

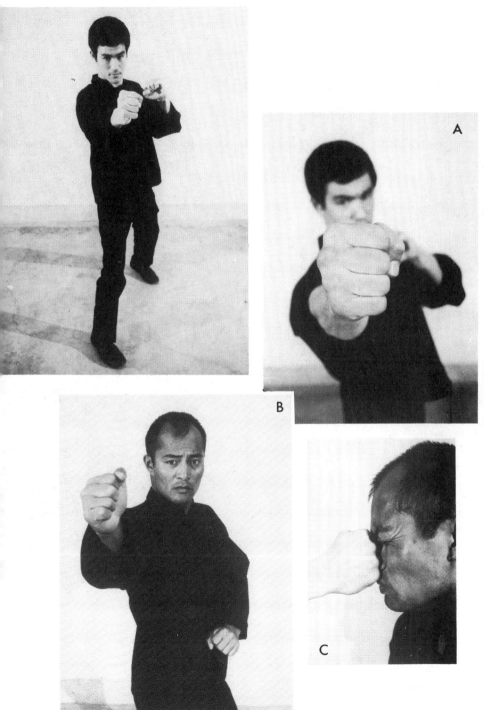

FRONT VIEW

SIDE VIEW

The straight right should be delivered directly from the on-guard position, as in photos 1 and 1A. Your hand should not telegraph your intention before delivery. Do not add extra movement such as withdrawing it just before delivery. The only motion

should come as a consequence of your slight weaving and bobbing
while you are looking for an opening or waiting to counter. Punch
straight out, as in photos 2 and 2A, with your fist in the
vertical position. Your rear hand should be in the guard position,

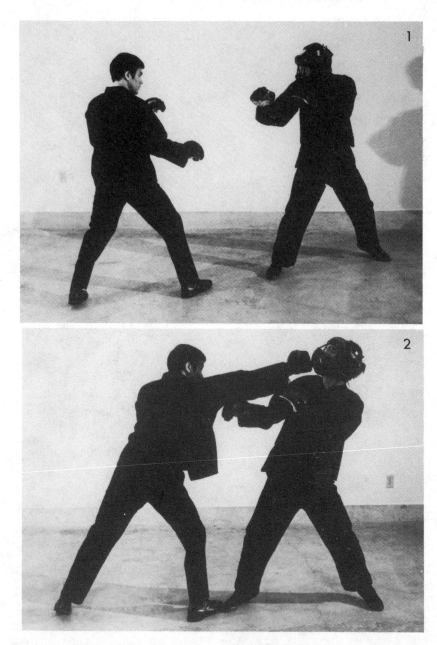

ready to block any blow. By putting your "shoulder" into the blow, you can increase your reach by as much as four inches and not reduce the impact of your punch, as long as you use your body properly and punch through, as in photos 3 and 3A (page 28).

Against someone standing closer to him, as in photo 1, Lee

delivers a quick, straight right without telegraphing, as in photo 2. But against someone standing further away, as in photo A, or who has the inclination to retreat, Lee penetrates a little deeper to launch his blow, as in photo B.

In all hand techniques, the hand moves before the foot. Delivery must be economical and from any angle and any distance. In an attack, the movements must be as concealing or as slight as ever, especially with your hands, to inhibit the opponent from reacting into a defensive or countering measure.

To be a master of attack you must understand that for every lead there is an opening, for each opening, a counter and for each counter, a block or parry. You must know when and how to use the lead with some security.

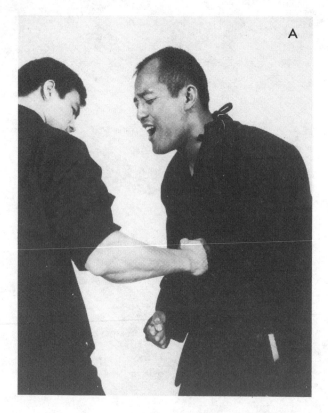

Lead to Body

Although the leading right to the body is not necessarily a heavy blow, it can be used effectively to bother your opponent and bring his guard down. If the punch is driven into the solar plexus, it can do real damage to the opponent, as in photo A.

THE LEAD TO THE BODY

FRONT VIEW 3

SIDE VIEW 3A

To execute the leading right to the body, stand in the on-guard position, as in photo 1 (front view) and 1A (side view). Then drop your body forward and step in, as in photos 2 and 2A. Your front leg should be slightly bent and your rear leg more

flexible. As you hit in an angle, your chin should naturally move into your right shoulder. At the full thrust, your rear hand should be guarding your face, as in photos 3 and 3A, and your weight should shift almost completely to your front foot.

It is important that you follow through with your punch. Try to sink your body to the level of the target so your blow will be delivered slightly upward or almost horizontally. This delivery position is safer and more effective.

Lee stands in the on-guard position against a right-lead opponent, as in photo 1. He moves in quickly with a blow to the midsection, simultaneously using his left hand to block a high lead punch, as in photo 2.

Most people are weak in the low line and blows toward that section are effective especially from disengagement. A disengage-

ment is a single movement of your hand passing from the line of engagement into the opposite line—throwing a hit from a closed line into an open line. Timing is very important, as you must start your attack as the opponent's arm is moving across or in the opposite direction.

Against a left-lead opponent, as in photo A, Lee feints with his lead hand to draw his opponent's hands upward, as in photo B. As soon as the opening develops, Lee drives a hard lead right to the solar plexus, as in photo C. He is now in position to deliver a combination of left and right.

To defend against a straight lead from a right stance, you can do several things: (1) keep your left hand open and hold it slightly

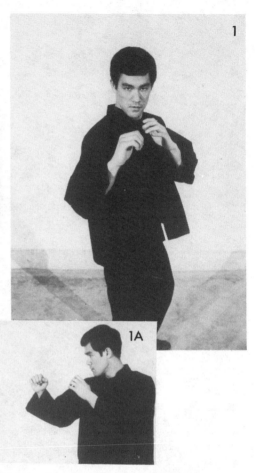

THE LEADING STRAIGHT LEFT

higher than normal, keeping it weaving. As the opponent's punch is launched toward your face, lean a little to your left and parry the blow with your left hand by slapping his wrist and forearm. No amount of strength is required to deflect even a powerful strike. The deflection will leave your opponent off-guard and off-balance for a quick counter to his face or body.

(2) Swing to your left by stepping in with your right foot and let go a hard right to the body or face. (3) Move to the right by stepping in with your right foot and throw a strong left to the body or head in a cross-counter. (4) Take a step back and counter as you move forward.

The Straight Left

The straight left is a powerful blow if delivered properly. It is

used as a counter or as a combination. The power is generated more than a lead punch because you are standing further away and can increase the momentum of the blow before contact. Furthermore, you have the full use of your body behind the punch.

But for most right-handers, using the left is unnatural, especially when thrown from a distance. To develop skill in punching with your left, practice with it constantly on the heavy bag until it is just as proficient as the other hand.

To throw a straight left, stand in the on-guard position, as in photos 1 and 1A. Rotate your hips clockwise, pivoting mostly on your flexed, rear foot, as in photos 2 and 2A. Your weight should shift to your front foot, and your lead hand is drawn toward your face for protection, as in photos 3 and 3A. Your punch should be delivered straight in front of your nose and not like photo X, which, after the delivery, leaves your upper line unguarded. Your target can be anywhere on your opponent's head, but the most vulnerable spot is the side of the jaw, as in photo Y. But do not aim at the head all the time. Sometimes drive through the opponent toward the center-line.

Against someone with the same stance (right lead), as in photo 1, Lee creates an opening by a feint, as in photo 2. First he throws a right by stepping out with his right foot. The opponent responds by raising his hands to meet the blow. Just before Lee's right connects, obstructing the opponent's sight, he delivers a

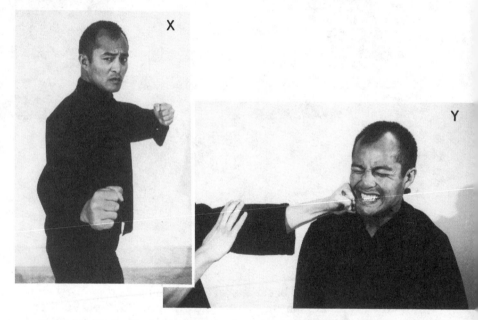

straight left to the opponent's face, as in photo 3. This delivery is done with a twist of his hip to the right as he pivots on the sole of his left foot. The pivot should be done sharply, with a snap of his hip, and completed with a snap of his left shoulder.

If your opponent steps back without parrying or blocking, it is often a good maneuver to renew the attack, aiming at the advanced target such as the shin or knee. It is also effective against someone who opens himself by retreating with wide movements or against one who tries to parry but is off-balance and is caught at the hesitation.

Against a fighter who places his weight on the rear foot instead of taking a short step back, attack that rear foot. The effectiveness of a renewed attack depends highly on your knowledge of the way your opponent fights. It can hardly succeed without preliminary plans. You must also have good footwork for a quick forward recovery and an ability to keep your opponent off-balance.

The techniques on a renewed attack can be a straight thrust and a feint, beat or trap with combinations. Attack by combination is usually comprised of set-ups. It is a series of punches or kicks delivered naturally and to more than one line. The purpose of the attack is to draw or force your opponent into a precarious position for a finishing blow.

Combination blows come in certain sequences. For instance, it is natural to punch first to the head and then to the body; a straight punch then a hook; a right hook then a straight left, or a straight left then a right jab.

There are also the triple blows in combinations. For instance, you can get to your opponent by sending two blows to his body after a slip. This generally results in your opponent dropping his guard and leaving an opening for the final blow.

There is also the "safety triple," in which the first blow and the final blow land at the same place. For example, if the initial punch is to the body and the second to his jaw, then the last punch should be to his body.

Often the left or rear thrust is used as a countering blow. This can be done by drawing your opponent to lead. When he does, you duck your head slightly and step inside his right lead, letting it slip over your left shoulder. Then throw your left punch with power by snapping your left shoulder. Keep your eyes constantly on his left hand and stop it with your right if he uses it.

Against someone in the opposite stance, as in photo 1, Lee feints with his right, as in photo 2, and then quickly delivers a straight left to the opponent's face, as in photo 3. Notice in photo 2, page 41, and photo 2, opposite page, that when the opponent stands in the opposite position from his, Lee doesn't have to penetrate too deeply.

Decoy or false attack is employed, not with the intention of hitting, but to draw or entice your opponent to attack in a specific line so you can parry the blow and counter. The attack is not a lunge but just a slight movement of the foot or body to create a response.

Chapter XIII
Hand Techniques for Offense
(part 2)

Right Strokes

It is not your lack of speed
  that you think you really need.

But many times it's your strokes
  that you use against all folks.

They may not be right for each fight
  so you are confused and too tight.

Learn and practice the right blows
  to fight better against all foes.

Although speed is important, too many fighters put too much emphasis on it. When a fighter fails in his offensive blows, many times he uses the wrong strokes and blames his failure to lack of speed.

A fighter must use the proper strokes at the right time against his opponent. To use the correct strokes, he has to study his opponent's style from different angles and study his tactics and timing. Included in this section are some of the strokes that are used in jeet kune do.

Straight Left to the Body

The straight left blow to the body, like the straight left, is powerful and can be used as a counter, used after a feint with the

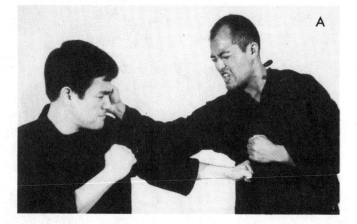

leading hand or even used in combination. Like the leading jab or leading straight, the body should follow the punch.

It is a punishing punch and can be applied with some safety because you are in a crouch position as you deliver the punch. Opportunity to use this punch is frequent because it is one of the best counters against an opponent who stands opposite to you, exposing his right side.

It is also effective in drawing your opponent's guard down and has been used triumphantly against tall fighters. This technique should be used primarily against an opponent who keeps his rear hand high to protect his face when delivering a lead punch.

The punch is delivered almost like the straight left except the blow is directed to the midsection area, as in photo A, or to

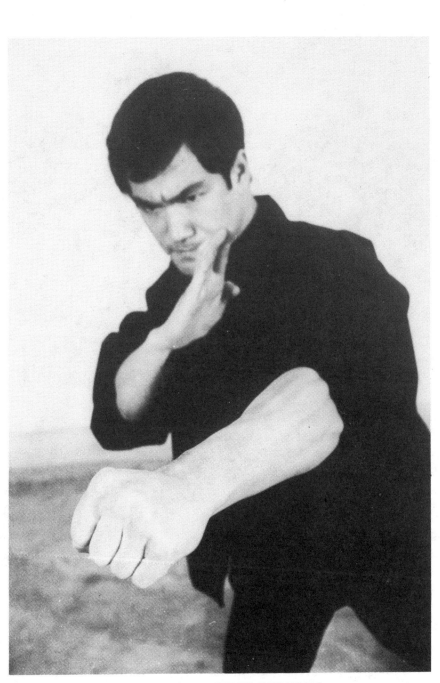

THE STRAIGHT LEFT TO THE BODY

the solar plexus. From an on-guard right lead position, as in photos 1 and 1A, bend your front knee slightly and keep your rear leg flexed, as in photos 2 and 2A. Your lead hand is drawn toward your face and now becomes the guard as you thrust your left hand. Your weight shifts to the front foot as you pivot on your back foot. For a more powerful blow, you can step slightly to the right as the blow is thrown. When returning to your posi-

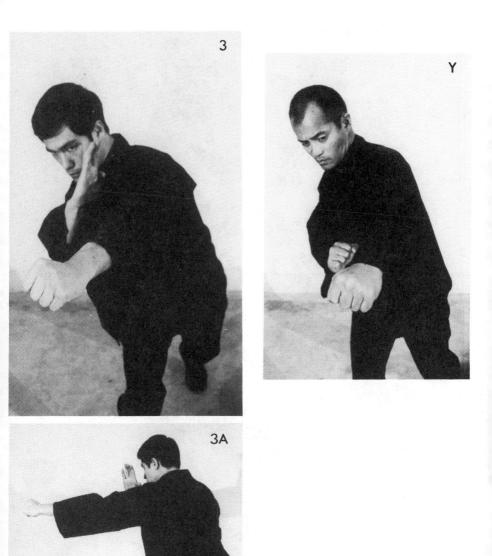

tion, keep your lead shoulder raised to protect against your opponent's left cross or left hook.

Meanwhile, your right or guard hand should be opened and placed close to your face by the time your thrust is completed, as in photos 3 and 3A. Sink your body so the blow can be thrown slightly upward or almost horizontal to your target. Don't use this punch, as in photo Y, exposing the upper line area.

Against an opponent in the right lead stance, as in photo 1, Lee creates an opening by a deep false attack, as in photo 2, drawing his opponent to raise his hands to meet the attack. Then he quickly sinks his body and smashes a left to the midsection, as in photo 3. The head is down along the left shoulder and well-protected against a counter.

Against an opponent who stands in the opposite position, as in photo A, Lee's penetration is not too deep. Instead, he feints a lead right at his face, as in photo B, at the same time stepping in closer. When the opponent commits himself to the feint, Lee

drives a hard straight left to his body, as in photo C. At this point, Lee's right hand is up and open and his elbow is down to guard against any counter.

Sometimes, instead of feinting to draw the opponent's lead, just wait for him to lead and quickly attack when there is an opening to his body. Body attack does have an advantage over head attack as your target is bigger and less mobile.

To stop a rear thrust to your body, just leave your front arm across your body and raise your lead shoulder in case your opponent throws a double hit or a "loop" punch.

Lead Jab

The jab is not a powerful punch but is used to keep your opponent off-balance, keeping him from being "set." It is a fast, snapping punch and not a push. Your hand should be held and return high to offset a rear-hand counter. The arms should be relaxed and should sink instead of pulling back when being brought back to the on-guard position.

It is practical to launch more than one jab because the second one has a good chance to land if the previous one is delivered with economy. The subsequent one is also a cover-up for a missed jab. A multitude of jabs can be thrown to keep your opponent on the defensive as you steadily press him, offering him no rest.

THE BACK FIST

Back Fist

The back fist is one of the most surprising punches you can deliver because it is fast, accurate and nontelegraphic. It can be launched from either the on-guard position or even when you are standing nonchalantly with your hands hanging loosely by your hips. At the latter position, you are in a nonbelligerent position to sneak a blow before your opponent can be prepared.

The delivery of the leading back fist should come directly from the front hand without telegraphing, as in photo X, and the blow should be coming overhand and not like photo Y, where the hand is swung horizontally because it was first withdrawn. The blow can be directed anywhere on your opponent's face but the temple is the best target, as in photo Z.

1

FRONT VIEW

1A

SIDE VIEW

From the on-guard position, as in photos 1 and 1A, the leading back fist is delivered in a vertical semicircular motion, as in photos 2 and 2A. Your bodyweight shifts to the front as your

rear hand simultaneously moves slightly downward to protect
against kicks as well as any punches to your head or body, as in
photos 3 and 3A. Open your rear hand for parrying.

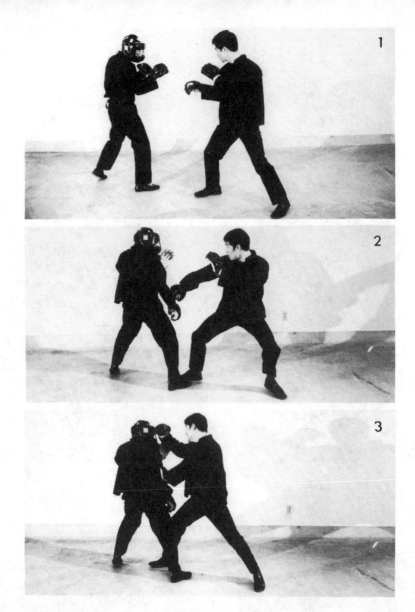

Against a right-lead-stance-opponent, as in photo 1, Lee traps the opponent's arm with his right and places his front foot on the opponent's right to prevent him from kicking, as in photo 2. Then he quickly switches his hands, using his left to immobilize the opponent's and his right to apply a back fist as he steps in, as in photo 3.

Against someone standing in the left-lead position, as in photo A Lee uses the same technique as in the prior illustration.

From the on-guard position he uses his right hand to trap the opponent's left, as in photo B, placing his lead foot next to the opponent's to prevent him from any countering kick. Then he moves in swiftly as he switches his hands, using his left for grabbing and his right to deliver a blow, as in photo C. Notice that Lee uses his left to jerk his opponent toward him as he simultaneously delivers a semicircular blow.

Trapping or immobilizing is a method of stopping your opponent from moving certain parts of his body and gives you safety as you launch your attack. For instance, one hand can be used for pinning and the other for striking. It can be used also as a protective maneuver when you are countering or slipping. Trapping is basically used to collide the line before engagement.

Trapping, deflecting, beating or engaging the hand of your opponent will cause him to contract or reduce his reaction, or force him to parry too soon or lose control of his performance. The foot can also be used to immobilize your opponent from kicking.

You can limit your opponent from executing a successful stop-hit if you will deflect or trap his hand while stepping forward. When trapping, you should cover your lines or use other means as guards and keep your movement tight. Also, as you are trapping or have already trapped your opponent's hand, use a stop-hit or time-hit if there is a disengagement.

The Hook Punch

The hook is a good countering or a follow-up blow because it is basically a short-range weapon, catching the opponent moving in. The lead hook can be used as a lead also when your opponent has failed to move out of your way. But usually this punch is used faster as a straight lead like a jab or after some other tactics. For instance, it can be used after feinting a cross, not too extreme, to obtain leverage and distance.

The hook should not be thrown in a wide, looping way but should be easy, snappy and loose. In loose hooking, the whip of the arm is the result of the body turning away from the arm until the play of the shoulder joint is used to the limit. Then the arm must follow the turning body. If done suddenly, this causes the arm to whip forward like an arrow from a bow.

The hand should not telegraph by withdrawing or lowering before delivery. It is not necessary to pull your hand back like many boxers. There is enough power without doing that if you use your footwork properly. Keep your lead heel raised outward so that the body can pivot easily. The weight of the body should shift to the opposite side from the punching hand. If you are throwing a lead hook, you must step in with the punch in order to contact.

In a lead hook, keep your rear hand high as a shield to your face and the rear elbow to protect your side. The hook should be thrown from an on-guard position to deceive your opponent and after it is completed, you should return to the same stance. Keep

Y

THE HOOK PUNCH

the lead shoulder high for full leverage when you hook to the side of the chin, as in photo Y.

Minimize your motion so that your action is just enough to have the maximum effect without hooking uncontrollably. If you exaggerate the outside hook, it will emanate into a swing, as in

photo X. You must keep it tight, as in photo Y. Besides, if you open a hook, you also reduce your defenses. The more sharply your elbow is bent, as in photo Z, the tighter and more explosive the hook. Keep your arm a little more rigid just before impact.

To deliver the hook from the on-guard position, as in photo 1, keep your rear guard high, as in photo 2, and your lead

heel raised outward to pivot with ease. Then rotate your hips swiftly counterclockwise as you deliver the hook, as in photo 3, shifting your weight to your rear foot. Throw the blow snappily with your concentration on speed. Like the other blows, drive your hook through the opponent. The most difficulty in the hook is to throw your punch with complete control of your body.

The lead hook should be used wisely. Against a clever defensive fighter, this may be the only way to penetrate his defense or open it up by forcing him to use other tactics. But the hook is mostly effective when you move in or move out. If you are against an opponent who throws an overreaching straight or swings, the hook is valuable.

Against an opponent in the same stance, as in photo 1, the lead hook is often delivered when he has lowered his rear hand guard, as in photo 2, or after he has thrown a lead jab. The punch is delivered with the weight on the rear foot, the hips rotating and the pivoting on the ball of the raised front foot, as in photo 3.

Against an opponent standing in the opposite position, as in photo A, Lee employs a false attack by crouching slightly and feinting a rear straight thrust, as in photo B. As the opponent drops his lead to block the punch, Lee retaliates with a high hook to his jaw, as in photo C.

The hook is a natural punch when combined with a sidestep.

You are moving obliquely and your direction facilitates an easy swing at the opponent. Paradoxically, when your opponent is side-stepping, a hook is the practical punch to deliver, too.

The lead hook is also good in close or in-fighting. The blow is thrown from the side or outside the opponent's range of vision. Besides, it can also go around the guard, an important offense especially after the opponent is shaken up by a straight blow.

The hook to the body is more damaging when in-fighting. Additionally, the body is an easier target—larger than the jaw and less mobile. To close in, feint to the head, then swiftly step forward with the front foot and throw your lead hook into his midsection or the nearest target. The groin is a good target because it is harder to block than, for instance, the jaw. When delivering the punch in close, duck to the opposite side of the hand that is throwing the hook. To do this, you have to bend your front knee so your shoulder will be almost the same level with the striking point. Retain your balance by keeping the toe of your back foot well extended. Keep your guard hand constantly close to your face.

Even though straight punches are recommended for medium-distance fighting, the hook should be used against an opponent who is blocking, evading or countering the straight punches. Vary your punches from high to low to high and from a single strike to combination.

The rear hook is an asset for close fighting, especially when you are breaking away or when the opponent is breaking away from you. This punch can also distract the opponent away from the lead hook.

The hook is mastered by training on a small, speed bag. Hit it sharply without twisting your body into distortion. To defend against it, do not move away from the opponent but move into the hook and let it pass around your neck.

Uppercut

The uppercut is used in close fighting. The blow, an upward scooping motion with the palm facing you, can be administered with either the lead or rear hand. The uppercut is almost useless against a fast, upright boxer who uses long lead jabs to your face. But it is a natural technique against someone who puts his head down and charges, swinging wildly.

To deliver the effective short uppercut, keep your knees bent before striking and straighten them as you throw the punch. At impact, you should be on your toes and leaning slightly backward. The weight should be on your left foot if the blow is a right and vice versa if the blow is a left.

Against a right lead opponent use your left hand to trap the opponent's right arm as you deliver a right lead uppercut. To execute the left rear uppercut, the lead hand is drawn back to protect your head and also to be prepared for countering. The left hand should be lowered so the inertia of the blow is across and up.

Chapter XIV
Attacks With Kicks

The Mighty Feet

If you are adept with your feet,
probably, you are hard to beat.

'Cause you can keep your foe at bay
with powerful kicks that can slay.

The shin-kick can stop an attack
while the side-kick can break his back.

The spin-kick can be a surprise
to bring your opponent down to size.

The sweep-kick is seldom used
'cause your foe can only be bruised.

For movies, it's a picturesque sight,
but for real, it has no might.

ATTACKS WITH KICKS

In attacking, the best kicks to use are the quick, fast ones. A kick has to be delivered before your opponent can defend against or move away from it. Be sure your opponent doesn't take advantage of your commitment. Attempt to psych your opponent with punishing blows, inflicting sharp pain.

In your training be aware of your delivery, landing and recovery. Use snapping kicks from the knee for more power and combine both knee and hip for more speed.

Learn to control your body so you can kick from high, low or ground level and while you are in motion—advancing, retreating, circling to the left or to the right.

Leading Shin and Knee Kick

It is natural for most martial artists to use or rely on their feet as the initial weapons in attacking. The leg is stronger and longer. In jeet kune do the low side kick to the shin or knee is used initially in the first encounter. The kick is explosive whether used in thrusting or snapping and can wreck the opponent's knee with one blow. It is a good technique to bridge the gap in order to employ combination. Even if the kick is not thrown excessively, it still can discourage an opponent from taking the initiative and keep him at a distance.

Against someone standing in the same stance, as in photo 1, Lee sweeps his lead hand upward to distract his opponent, as in photo 2, and quickly lunges forward to deliver his low side kick to the knee, forcing him to the ground, as he continues to thrust without letting up; as in photo 3. Notice how far Lee stands from his opponent when the kick is delivered, as in photo 3.

THE LEADING KNEE KICK

Against someone standing opposite, as in photo 1, Lee uses the same approach by sweeping his hand upward, as in photo 2, and quickly drives his side kick to the left knee this time, as in photo 3. Notice that Lee approaches his opponent with his eyes upon the face and not on the target area. He does this to camouflage his intention—keeping his opponent guessing.

THE LEADING SIDE KICK

Leading Side Kick

The side kick is the most powerful blow in JKD. It is so strong that many times, even a block will not prevent it from knocking or hurting your opponent. The kick can be launched from a medium distance but there is more power if it is launched from farther out, as you can increase your momentum before contact.

Against someone in the same stance, as in photo 1, Lee raises his hand from a medium distance, as in photo 2, keeping his other hand down to protect from a countering kick. He quickly

delivers a side kick to the opponent's rib-section, as in photo 3,
hurling him backward, as in 4. Although the kick is powerful, it
is quite difficult to hit your opponent solidly if he is a defensive

fighter. The defensive measures are either to move away far enough from the penetration or sidestep from the kick. Another way is to parry the blow with a chance of grabbing it.

Against someone in the same stance, as in photo 1, Lee just

moves in, studying the reaction of the opponent, as in 2. When the opponent starts to back off from the attack, Lee lunges without any hesitation, as in photo 3. Moving faster than the opponent, Lee delivers his side kick, as in photo 4.

In the series of photos, opposite page, as the opponent stands in the opposite stance, as in photo 1, Lee tries his familiar hand-raised feint as he moves forward, as in photo 2. But this time the opponent refuses to respond so Lee changes his tactics and uses a high side kick, over the opponent's guarding hands, to the face, as in photo 3.

THE HOOK KICK

Hook Kick

The hook kick is the most dominating kick in JKD because it is easy to hit your opponent—the way the kick is delivered gives you more opportunity than others—and at the same time, offers you security from a medium-distance fighting. It can be delivered quickly and is very versatile. It can be aimed at the head, midsection and even the groin.

Against a right-lead-stance-opponent, as in photo 1, Lee first feints a knee kick, drawing the guarding hand down, as in photo 2. Once the opponent reacts to the feint, Lee sends a high hook kick to his face, as in photos 3 and 3A (bird's-eye view).

The feint must be impressive enough to create a response from the opponent. The number of feints should be limited to be effective. It is risky to try an attack with more than two feints. The more complicated the maneuvers of the compound attack, the less

3A

the probability of success.

The feint is one method of gaining distance. Your first feint should shorten at least one-half the distance between you and your opponent. Your next motion should cover the last half of the distance. Your feint should be prolonged to give your opponent ample time to react. But not too long so he has time to block your attack. You have to be just ahead of it. All your motions should be slight, just enough for a response.

In this next series of encounters against an opponent with a right lead stance, as in photo 1, Lee tries the raising hand distraction to open up the midsection area, as in photo 2. When the opponent responds to the bluff, Lee delivers a hook kick to his left side, as in photo 3.

Against an opponent in the opposite stance, as in photo A, Lee lowers his body, as in photo B, and fakes a low hook kick to draw the opponent's left hand to protect his low line area, as in photo C. When he does, Lee delivers a high hook kick to his head, as in photo D. This hook kick is easier to execute against someone in the same stance as yours.

THE SPIN KICK

1

The Spin Kick

The spin kick is used cautiously in jeet kune do because against a defensive or less aggressive fighter, you may be caught with your back to him while you are turning. But nevertheless, it is a valuable kick against an unwary opponent who keeps on rushing.

The spin kick is one of the most difficult to perform because it can leave you out-of-balance while revolving. Hitting the target can be a problem too because for a moment you have to take your eyes from it and still hit it while your body is turning.

The spin kick is used mostly as a counter but from time to time it can be used as an attack to surprise your opponent. Against someone in the same stance, as in photo 1, Lee sweeps his hand upward to distract as he moves toward his opponent. Then at the right range, he pivots on his right foot and rotates his body suddenly, as in photo 2. He tries to keep his eyes on his opponent to judge his distance. Before the opponent can react, he delivers a spin kick to his midsection, as in photo 3. Some martial artists

employ the spin kick in a sweeping or slapping motion so the blow is projected from the side. But in JKD it is more a thrust, with the blow hitting directly in front of the target.

To apply a high spin kick against his opponent in the same

stance, as in photo 1, Lee fakes with his lead hand, as in photo 2. But the opponent doesn't respond to the gesture in photo 2, so Lee quickly pivots on his right foot and sends a high kick to his face, as in photo 3, driving him back, as in photo 4.

Against someone in the opposite stance, as in photo 1, Lee sweeps his hand, as in photo 2, and quickly turns his body completely, as in photo 3, to drive a spin kick between the opponent's guards, forcing him off his feet, as in photo 4.

Although the spin kick works best against an unwary, aggressive type of fighter, sometimes it is also very effective against a fighter who doesn't expect it. In JKD this is one of the few times the left foot is used for kicking from the on-guard position.

THE SWEEP KICK

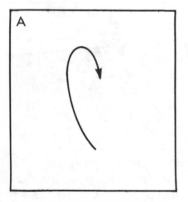

A

THE PATH OF THE FOOT

3

Sweep Kick

The sweep or reverse kick is seldom used in JKD because, against someone in the same stance as you, the lead hand is always protecting his face. Second, the kick is delivered high and is apt to be caught against an experienced fighter. Third, the kick is not powerful enough to knock your opponent down.

The sweep kick has its effectiveness against an unwary fighter who tends only to protect his left side while standing in the right lead position. It is one of the few kicks that will penetrate against a fighter who habitually leaves his lead foot high above the ground to jam while attacking.

Against someone in the same stance, as in photo 1, Lee begins to deliver a sweep kick, as in photo 2. The delivery of the kick is similar in this case to a front kick and deceives the opponent who attempts a low block. Unencumbered, the kick finds its target, as in photo 3. The path of the kick is from left to right in a semicircular motion, as in diagram A.

2   1

Against an opponent in the opposite stance, as in photos 1 and 1A (bird's-eye view), Lee moves in such a way that the opponent thinks he is about to send a side kick to his midsection, as in

photos 2 and 2A. While the opponent anticipates the side kick, Lee reaches his face by driving his foot above the guarding hand, as in photos 3 and 3A.

Chapter XV

Defense and Counter

Countering

*Countering may look like a defense
   but it's an advanced form of offense.*

*Countering is a crafty strategy
   and requires real art in fighting.*

*Countering can keep your opponent edgy
   especially while you are waiting.*

*Countering is best when he's leading
   because he cannot do much guarding.*

DEFENSE AND COUNTER

Counterattacking is a crafty maneuver. It is quite safe to use and can be very damaging to your opponent because he is generally caught moving in.

Second, if you are matched against someone equally as skilled as you, you have the advantage because your opponent is bound to expose more of himself as he is leading and committing himself. In the meantime, you are remaining in the on-guard stance, waiting for the opening. It is preferable to feint your opponent to lead instead of waiting for him to take the initiative.

The art of counterattacking can be applied after provoking your opponent to attack or drawing and luring him by leaving yourself purposely open. The idea of counter is to avoid the blow and hit your opponent while he is out of balance or not in position to guard himself.

Countering requires real proficiency in the art of fighting. Actually it is an advanced form of offense. For each lead, there are numerous counters but you should select the most effective one instantly. This can only be done by constant practice until you are conditioned to react spontaneously.

After countering, follow up by pressing your opponent until he is down or until he retaliates. Be careful of an opponent who uses the double hit. His first blow is used to entice you and his second blow will be the real one, as you attempt to counter.

Leading Finger Jab

The leading finger jab is a good defensive and countering weapon to stop an attack before it unfolds and as a consequence, it frustrates your opponent. It is easy to employ and is quick—so quick, that the opponent gets it in his eye before he can deliver his punch. It is thrown with your fingers outstretched, an added extension of your hand.

THE LEADING FINGER JAB

It is a good stop-hit weapon and you should use it at every opportunity during the course of fighting. It enables you not only to score effectively and create openings but it can quickly demoralize an aggressive and confident opponent.

Lee was a skillful exponent of the stop-hit. Here, he shows how to use it against an opponent standing in the opposite stance, as in

photo 1. Lee quickly moves in as he sees the opponent's swing coming, as in photo 2. With his lead hand, which only has to travel a much shorter distance than a swing, Lee thrusts it toward his opponent's face, as in photo 3. Lee constantly keeps his guard hand high to block, as in photo 4.

A stop-hit must be correctly timed just as the opponent begins his attack. The idea is to anticipate and intercept the attacker in his path and at the same time deliver a blow, keeping yourself secured by being out of the attacker's reach or by the use of other covering. Success depends on proper anticipation and timing as well as hitting the target perfectly.

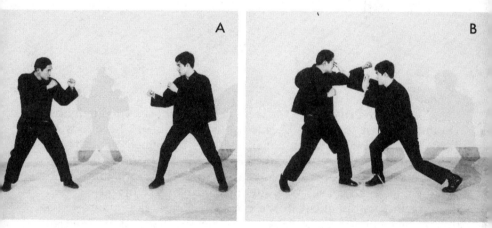

An effective maneuver against a swinging opponent is to counter-time into his action or stop-kick into his advanced target or exposed areas.

In the sequence above, against someone in the opposite stance, as in photo A, Lee prepares for the attack. As soon as his opponent is about to deliver a straight lead, Lee quickly intercepts the blow and continues with his right finger jab to the opponent's eye, as in photo B. He keeps his rear hand high to protect against any countering. Timing is so important in the attack on development. After anticipating your opponent's line of attack, you intercept his arm or foot and counter, just as he is about to deliver.

THE LEADING RIGHT

Leading Right

The leading right, like the leading finger jab, is a good defensive punch against the swing because your blow doesn't have to travel too far. Even when the opponent initiates the punch, you can beat him to his delivery. Besides, against a wild swinger or a slow-moving fighter, you can really frustrate and disturb him by not allowing him to get set, by your constant blows to his face.

Against an opponent in the opposite stance, as in photo 1, Lee counters with a straight right lead as the opponent attempts a right swing, as in photo 2. Lee stops the attack when his punch contacts the face, as in photo 3.

Actually, the stop-hit is used to arrest the attack as it is unfolding. It can be an indirect or direct attack. It may be used while the opponent steps forward to punch or kick, while he is feinting, or while he is moving between a complication combination.

Against someone standing in the opposite stance, as in photo A, who attempts a swing with his left lead, Lee counters quickly, as in photo B. He counters when he sees the opponent draw his hand to launch his attack.

Often it is necessary to step or lean forward to employ an effective stop-hit—beyond the opponent's focus. Besides, without taking a step, you may not beat him to the punch.

Shin or Knee Kick

The shin or knee low side kick, sometimes referred to as the "stop" kick, is one of the most formidable defensive tactics in JKD. If done proficiently, you can just about stop any kind of attack against the punch or kick. The concept of this kick is to beat your man to the attack. That means you have to stop your opponent while he is in motion, just before acceleration or just before he attacks. To do that, you must be much quicker than he is. This trait can be developed by training heavily in the science of awareness or the art of anticipation.

THE KNEE KICK

As mentioned in a prior chapter, Bruce Lee was always a step ahead of his opponent because of his keen, cultivated awareness. He used to practice it constantly to increase his sensitivity of his mobile surrounding.

To employ the low side kick against someone standing in the same position, as in photo 1, Lee studies his opponent's face, waiting for his first move. As soon as the opponent begins his attack, as in photo 2, Lee sweeps his lead hand upward to initiate his momentum. Before his opponent can land his blow, Lee retaliates with a low side kick to his knee, as in photo 3.

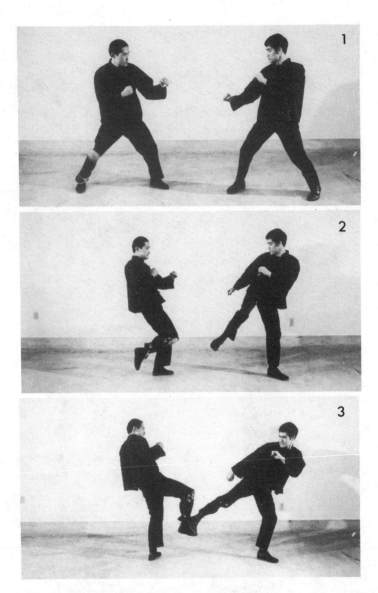

If the opponent is in the opposite stance, as in photo 1, and is planning to use his back foot to deliver a front kick, as in photo 2, Lee quickly meets the attack with his lead foot lifted above the floor to intercept the opponent's kicking foot in mid-air, as in photo 3. You must realize that the stop-kick is not necessarily a countering blow but sometimes used strictly to stop or block an offensive maneuver.

An opponent who fights from a crouching position is easier to

handle because of his limited maneuverability, as in photo A. His low stance and extended feet restrict him from attacking and retreating quickly. In photo B, Lee just moves away from the right lead punch thrown by his opponent. Lee was able to move away easily from the punch because a low-stance fighter has to telegraph his movement whenever he tries to stand upright to move forward or backward. After avoiding the blow, Lee delivers a crushing shin kick, as in photo C.

Fighting an opponent who stands on the opposite stance as in photo 1, is not different from one whose feet are in the same position as yours. Probably it is easier to jam his lead leg because it is aligned with yours. In photo 2, when the opponent lunges at Lee, he meets the attack directly. Even with the opponent having a head start, Lee's quick reaction stops the attack from materializing, as in photo 3.

Against an opponent in a closer range, as in photo A, and who stands in the opposite position, Lee evades a left lead punch and simultaneously delivers a kick to the lead knee, as in photo B. This is a fairly safe countering move because the leg has a longer reach than the hand.

Side Stop-Kick

The side stop-kick is almost like the low shin and knee kick except that the latter kick is employed more devastatingly as the kick is directed higher. The side stop-kick is used not only to stop the attack but also to knock the opponent down.

The kick is used extensively in JKD because it can be used in medium and far-distance fighting. Besides, it is the most powerful blow. When delivered properly, you need just one kick to completely stop an opponent.

Against an opponent standing in the opposite position at a

THE SIDE STOP-KICK

lengthy distance, as in photo 1, Lee is in a secure position and has more time to prepare for an attack, as in photo 2. After studying the opponent's approach, he moves toward him and unleashes a punishing side kick to his chest, as in photo 3. The impact from the kick not only stops the attack but drives the opponent backward to the floor, as in photo 4.

Proper timing and distance are important in the application of an effective stop-hit. When the distance is wide, the opponent generally needs some kind of planning in his attack. At this moment, you should launch your attack.

A smart fighter doesn't attack until he initially attains control of the opponent's timing or hand position. He endeavors to draw the stop-hit by any method to bring his opponent's hand and leg within range in order to control it.

Usually the stop-hit is employed with a straight thrust or kick, but it may be used in a disengagement or counter-disengagement or while ducking and slipping.

From a middle distance, Lee quickly stop-hits an opponent who

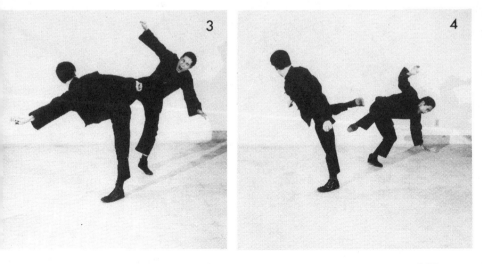

attempts to kick with his rear foot, as in photo 1. Once the attack is launched, Lee, without any hesitation, counters by sliding his rear foot forward and employs a right side kick to the opponent's chest, as in photo 2. The hard blow sends the opponent reeling backward, as in photo 3.

Against an onrushing assault from a middle distance, as in photo A, Lee moves into his opponent as he sees a right swing coming. With a quick lunge—not too deep, as the opponent is closing in—Lee lets go a powerful side kick, as in photo B. The blow stops the attack and drives the opponent backward, as in photo C.

A stop-hit is an excellent defense against an opponent who attacks wildly without any kind of covering or against one who stands too near. Sometimes you have to angle your body to find the opening and to control the opponent's hand.

Against an opponent who is in the opposite stance, as in photo 1, and who moves cautiously from a close distance, Lee carefully waits for the attack. As soon as his opponent moves in with a straight left, Lee steps slightly away, just enough to avoid the blow, as in photo 2.

Then he quickly shifts his footing and utilizes a right side kick, as in photo 3. The kick must be delivered with his body erect or

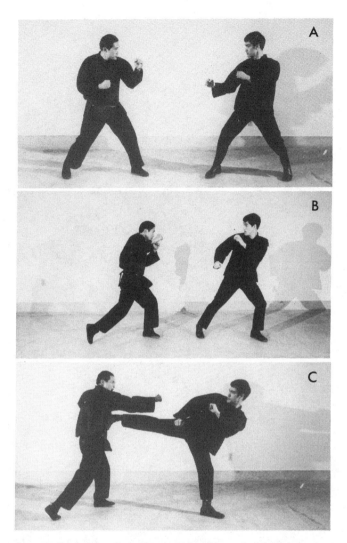

moving forward. Otherwise, there is no force behind it.

Another way to score is to use a direct or simple attack when the opponent is within distance and he doesn't retreat with his parry. To be certain, hit him when he is stepping forward into range, while he is shifting his weight forward or indicates "weightiness."

In another close-distance fighting, Lee again waits for the opponent's initial action, as in photo A. As soon as the opponent commits himself, Lee steps back slightly, readying both hands against an unexpected blow, as in photo B. Then he counters with a side kick as he regains his balance, as in photo C.

THE HOOK KICK

1

Sometimes it is wise to induce your opponent to stop-hit fully, preventing him from recovering against a parry and a counterattack. But be aware, so that he doesn't feint a stop-hit to draw you into a trap.

Hook Kick

The hook kick is one of the fastest and quickest kicks in jeet kune do and is used mainly as an offensive weapon. It can be launched swiftly without "telegraphing" the delivery. It is a good offensive and countering kick. It lacks power, when compared to the side kick, but it can be used very effectively. It is targeted at your opponent's vulnerable spots.

Against an onrushing attack, as in photo 1, Lee quickly pivots on his rear foot and switches his weight to it, avoiding the rush by moving away from the path of the attack but still maintaining his balance, as in photo 2. He stops the attack with a high hook kick to the face, as in photo 3.

Against a cautious fighter who stands from a middle distance, as in photo 1, Lee fakes a right punch to his face, as in photo 2. As the opponent commits himself with his own straight right, Lee parries and almost in one smooth motion, seizes the opponent's right wrist. Then he quickly lets go a hook kick to his groin, as in photo 3.

This is referred to as the sequence of attack on completion. After the opponent has lunged, you parry his blow and divert his primary attack. Then you counter while the opponent's body is extended from the lunge or during his act of recovery—there is no movement of your opponent's foot during this brief phase.

Against someone using the compound preparation, whereby he steps forward and employs his hand simultaneously, economical trapping is useful to either immobilize or create a reaction so you can punch or kick.

THE SPIN KICK

Spin Kick

· The spin kick is a surprise countering tactic. It is not recommended to be used as an offensive or attacking weapon. It is a

difficult kick to master, but once you are adept in using it, it may be your best weapon against a skilled opponent.

The spin kick should be used sparingly and mostly against an aggressive straight-line fighter, who constantly rushes at you. It is difficult to employ against a countering and defensive opponent.

Lee and his opponent stand at a far distance, feeling each other out, as in photo 1. Suddenly, his opponent rushes forward as Lee

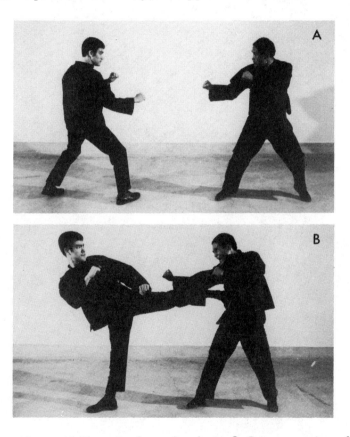

prepares to meet the attack, as in photo 2. Lee, a master of the spin kick, delivers a perfect kick to his face with ease, as in photo 3.

Standing in the middle distance, Lee faces a cautious opponent, as in photo A. Normally, a spin kick is not the tactic to use here, but Lee applies it effectively, as in photo B. This may work if the opponent is unwary or is a slow-reacting fighter.

Chapter XVI

Attributes and Tactics

Tactic

Tactic is for the intelligent
    who's a step ahead of his opponent.

He uses his brains in a fight
    while another can't see the light.

He varies his tactic with each foe,
    with punches and kicks thrown high and low.

He studies his opponent with care
    and fights with judgment and dare.

Tactic alone can't insure success;
    attitude is part of the process.

A fighter with great confidence
    plans his encounter with good sense.

ATTRIBUTES AND TACTICS

Speed

A person must have certain attributes in order to be a skilled fighter. The attributes may be learned or innate. For instance, speed is an innate trait but can also be developed further. If you are born without speed then you have to practice daily to acquire it or if you do have speed but want to increase it, you must train also.

There are several different types of speed. A perceptual speed is the quickness of your eyes to see an opening through the action or inaction of your opponent.

Mental speed is the ability of your mind to select rapidly the right techniques to attack or counter against an opponent. Performance speed is your ability to accelerate your body, feet or hands from a starting or set position and continue to increase the speed once your body or parts are in motion.

Then there is the alteration speed, which is the ability to change direction quickly in midstream—capability of altering the direction while in flight.

Speed is a confusing attribute. It comprises several elements such as your mobility, spring or resilience, stamina, physical and mental alertness—time needed to recognize and time needed to react. The more complex the situation, the slower you tend to react, as it takes your mind a longer time to comprehend.

The following aspects are needed to attain greater speed: (1) warming-up exercise to reduce viscosity and increase your flexibility; (2) a suitable stance; (3) visual and audial awareness, and (4) quick reacting habitual patterns.

Vision awareness or keen perceptual speed must be learned through constant practice as it isn't inherited. It should be part of your daily training—just a short, concentrated practice to perceive rapidly. But this should be supplemented with longer training outside of the dojo, as explained in Chapter V of *Basic Training*.

When your perception is directed on a simple concept such as hearing a gun go off or the dropping of a flag, your probability of improving your perceptual speed becomes less. The reason is that you can react almost to your full capacity to a simple act. But you can improve upon the preparatory movement to shorten the responding time. In other words, your improvement of keen awareness can shorten your reaction time.

The following reasons can lengthen your reaction time: (1) if you are exceptionally emotional; (2) when you are tired; (3) when you are not trained, and (4) when you lack concentration.

Choice reaction requires more comprehension and deliberation than simple reaction which is instinctive, quickest and most accurate. Like speed, if you have to concentrate on more than one item or act, your reaction will be slower as each requires some degree of concentration before you can respond.

During training you should reduce unnecessary choice reactions and if possible present your opponent with a variety of probable responses, forcing him to a slower, choice-reaction position.

Your opponent's reaction time is lengthened when the stimuli are combined: when he is inhaling, when he has just completed his technique, when his attention or perception are distracted and when he is off-balance.

A person who is slow in responding and in delivering can overcome this disadvantage through quick perceiving. An offensive fighter, who can use only his right foot and right hand extensively, should learn to use both hands and both feet. Displaying a one-sided offense allows his defensive opponent the quicker response, as his concentration area is being confined.

Attitude

An athlete with a "winning attitude" is self-confident and relaxed. He feels himself in command of the situation. He may also experience a psychological effect of nervousness, "butterflies in the stomach," nausea and may even vomit before the event; a condition which is quite natural among novices as well as many experienced athletes.

Once he is in the ring or on the field, he is able to control his emotions and perform at his highest peak. But a novice or a champion who is so intent on winning may continue to be so tense that his muscles begin to work against him. He becomes stiff and his motion becomes awkward.

A fighter must not take a lackadaisical attitude. He should learn to compete and practice at full speed continuously and not just perform moderately with the idea that he can increase the tempo at any time. A real competitor trains and competes at top capacity—harder and faster than normally required. He develops a good mental attitude.

Experience has shown that an athlete can perform to his capacity as long as needed. His latent energy or "second wind" does come into play if he performs at his limit.

But the experienced and older athletes do not waste their energy either. A great athlete conserves his energy by using his skill more effectively. He employs fewer wasteful motions—economy of motion.

To improve performance, momentum should be used to a minimum if it takes great muscular effort. Instead, momentum should be utilized to overcome resistance. You should understand that curved motions demand less effort than straight-line movements, when your direction has to change suddenly and sharply.

You must understand that it is a natural tendency to over-mobilize or over-exert your effort when confronted by an unfamiliar task. You should train with an easy and natural rhythm so your performance will be smooth and automatic. When your initiating muscles are not restricted, your movements will be more accurate and easier.

To become a champion requires a good mental attitude toward preparation. You have to accept the most tedious task with pleasure. The better prepared you are to respond to a stimulus, the more satisfaction you will find in the response. The less prepared, the more irritated you will feel when you have to perform.

Tactics

A fighter can be classified either as a mechanical or an intelligent fighter. The mechanical fighter fights in a similar pattern in each encounter. His strokes are repetitious and automatic.

An intelligent fighter will alter his tactics in order to use the right strokes, depending on his opponent's technique and the way he fights. He approaches each encounter with strategy based upon preliminary analysis, preparation and execution.

The preliminary analysis is made during the initial encounter. It consists of studying your opponent's habits, weaknesses and strengths. Is he aggressive or is he defensive? His dominant offenses and defenses? You may have to use false attacks to compel him to reveal his speed, reaction and skill.

Preparation comes after understanding your opponent's fighting ability. You now have at least a plan to outwit your opponent, taking advantage of his weakness. If you are planning to take the offense, you must control the situation. You may mislead him with false attacks followed by the real attacks—varying your attacks to keep your opponent confused and occupied so he can't assume the initiative. You must be prepared to parry if your opponent attempts a surprise stop-hit or counter.

Although the preparation and attack form one smooth motion, they should really be two separate movements to prepare you against a possible counterattack.

You should be able to halt rapidly and effortlessly when advancing for the preparation of attack. Pay close attention to your balance and foot movement. Short, rapid steps are easier to control than lengthy ones.

Often, especially in close fighting, you can attack on the preparation or arrest your opponent's motion before he can conceive or materialize his plan. This generally includes some movements to deflect the opponent's lead or cause a reaction for an opening when the feints failed. It also allows a change of distance.

Attack by preparation can also be applied against an opponent who maintains an accurate distance and thereby is difficult to reach, as he secures his position by staying constantly out of attacking distance. To reach him, you have to draw him into range by taking a short step back.

If you repeat the attack by preparation too often, it will attract a stop-hit rather than a parry. So initiate it with great economy, eliminating or shortening the time of vulnerability, and just opening the lines enough to trap. Practice preparations during engagement, change of engagement and feints on your partner.

Execution of your real attack demands surprise, quickness, fluidity and good timing. Your thought must be decisive, alert and pragmatic. If your opponent seizes the initiative, you may regain it by disturbing his concentration through constant intimidations of counterattacking, by attacking his outside line or by beating his guard.

Tactics are the ability to think a step ahead of your opponent. This requires good judgment, ability to see the openings, skill in anticipation, and "guts." Mechanical ability is a must to carry out your strategy. But mechanical perfection alone does not ensure success. You must be able to use your technical ability with intelligent analysis of your opponent.

A good fighter first controls his distance with superior footwork and then continues to lead the opponent's rhythm with feints, false attacks and short but effective hittings.

Learn to use your own rhythm to confuse your opponent then surprise him with a burst of quickness. Another effective method is to use the broken-time attack, a slight pause just before the impact. This will disrupt the opponent's defense.

A novice's rhythm, likewise, may be hard to judge because of its irregularity. A beginner also may not be able to follow your lead. He may panic and parry too soon in a form of an uncontrolled whip with no direction and accidentally catch your arm. To avoid this, learn to be patient and only use simple, or direct attack swiftly when there is an opening. Refrain from using the compound attacks.

A novice's irregular rhythm may come as a broken-rhythm attack unintentionally or may fool even the more skilled fighters who do not expect such a rhythm. In such a case, keep your distance and let your clumsy opponent overreach before countering.

A clever fighter does not fight the same way against all his opponents. He varies his tactics with direct and complex attacks and counters. He also alters his distance and position against each opponent.

One rule is not to use complicated techniques unless they are necessary to achieve your goal. First, use simple movements and if they don't work, then introduce the more complex ones. Simple attack from the on-guard position will often catch your opponent off-guard, especially after a series of false attacks and feints. The defender expects a complex action or a preparation and is not ready for the swift and nontelegraphic blow. To connect against a good fighter with a combination is gratifying and reveals your knowledge of techniques, but to hit him with a simple and direct blow shows your great proficiency in your ability.

Half of your fight is won if you know what your opponent is doing. Against a calm, patient fighter who protects himself well while in the ready position, who avoids any preparation and who stays out of range, do not attack directly. Such a fighter is normally well-versed in hitting and stop-kicking. Against such a fighter, draw his stop-hit with good feints then retaliate with trapping or grappling. Your feints should be longer.

But against a nervous fighter, your feint should be shorter. You should agitate a nervous fighter but remain relaxed against both the nervous and calm fighters.

A shorter man has the inclination to attack the advanced targets to overcome his shorter reach. He prefers closed fighting if he is stronger. Against such an opponent, fight without touching or extending your on-guard position to disturb and restrict his strategy.

A tall fighter is usually slower but has longer reach which can do damage. Against such a fighter, keep a safe distance until you can close in. Also keep your distance against a fighter who continues to use renewed attacks or keeps on advancing. But do not constantly step back on the attacks, as this is what he wants you to do. Instead, you should step forward into his attack to unbalance his maneuver.

It is important that you always reverse the tactics used by your opponent. For instance, use counters against one who likes to use stop-hits and use stop-hits against an opponent who uses feints. Box a fighter and fight a boxer. But ironically it is not smart to constantly attack a defensive opponent.

Awkward fighters use exaggerated and unexpected movements. Against such a fighter, stand at a distance and parry at the last instant. Because his attacks are simple and direct, your most effective weapon is a stop-hit or a time-hit.

Use renewed attack with a quick lunge upon an opponent who has the tendency to withdraw his hand or foot when a blow is launched toward it. Often a series of high feints will open the low-line areas, especially around the knee and shin.

During real combat, keep your eyes glued on your opponent. In close fighting, watch his lower line to protect your face and in far-distance fighting, watch his eyes. Keep him on the defensive and keep him guessing. Strike from all angles and press him once you have him in trouble. Draw him to step forward and when he does, attack him. Concentrate your attacks on his weaknesses and make him fight "your fight," not his.

The difference between an amateur and an expert is that when an expert sees an opportunity, he seizes it quickly. He makes use of his arsenal and intelligence, delivering punches and kicks in a well-thought-out manner—creating opening after opening until he delivers a powerful, damaging blow.

More Bruce Lee Books from Ohara

TAO OF JEET KUNE DO
by Bruce Lee. Code No. 401

BRUCE LEE'S FIGHTING METHOD Vol. 1: Self-Defense Techniques
by Bruce Lee and M. Uyehara. Code No. 402

BRUCE LEE'S FIGHTING METHOD Vol. 2: Basic Training
by Bruce Lee and M. Uyehara. Code No. 403

BRUCE LEE'S FIGHTING METHOD Vol. 3: Skill in Techniques
by Bruce Lee and M. Uyehara. Code No. 404

BRUCE LEE'S FIGHTING METHOD Vol. 4: Advanced Techniques
by Bruce Lee and M. Uyehara. Code No. 405

CHINESE GUNG FU
by Bruce Lee. Code No. 451

THE LEGENDARY BRUCE LEE
by the Editors of Black Belt magazine. *Code No. 446*

THE BRUCE LEE STORY
by Linda Lee. Code No. 460

THE INCOMPARABLE FIGHTER
by M. Uyehara. Code No. 461

OHARA [ ] PUBLICATIONS, INC., 24715 Ave. Rockefeller, P.O. Box 918, Santa Clarita, CA 91380-9018